A Camp in the Bush

By Eliza Webb

I'm camping with my mates!

Our bush camp coaches are Brook and Neil.
They'll teach us lots of bush camping skills.

Neil will help us make a den at the foot of a tree.

We pick up long sticks of wood for the frame.

We put branches from bushes on the frame of the den.

It will look so good!

Our den looks great!

It's cosy inside.

Then we look for some small sticks and twigs.

Brook teaches us how to make a fire nook from rocks.

We put the sticks and twigs in it.

We stand back while Brook makes the fire.

It's time to cook!

Neil puts a pot full of beans on the fire to cook.

We'll enjoy those beans!

Neil pulls some cookies out of his bag!

He puts sweet goodies inside. Then he'll toast them.

We don't want to sleep yet, so we read from Neil's book of camp tales.

Then Brook puts the fire out.

We put our thick sleeping bags into our tents.

Bush camp is good fun!

CHECKING FOR MEANING

1. Where did the campers make their den? *(Literal)*
2. What food did Neil cook over the fire? *(Literal)*
3. Why did the campers put the sticks and twigs into the nook? *(Inferential)*

EXTENDING VOCABULARY

foot	What is the foot of a tree? Why do you think it is called that?
nook	What is a nook? Is it a big space or a small space? Which words in the book rhyme with the word *nook*?
tales	What is a tale? What is another word the author could have used instead of *tale*?

MOVING BEYOND THE TEXT

1. People often go camping in groups as a way to stay safe in the bush. Why might it be unsafe to go camping in the bush alone?
2. The kids in this book camped in the bush. Where else might people go camping?
3. What kinds of things might you do when camping that you wouldn't do at home?
4. The campers and coaches worked together to set up the camp. Tell me about a time you've worked together with someone to get something done.

TIME TO WRITE

Write a short story that might be found in Neil's book of camping tales.

PRACTICE WORDS

wood
looks
pulls
foot
look
good
cookies
Brook
bushes
cook
bush
put
full
puts
don't
nook
goodies
they'll
we'll
book
he'll
I'm
it's